Metamorphosis

Breanna Troutman

BookLeaf Publishing
India | USA | UK

Made with ❤ on the BookLeaf Publishing Platform
www.bookleafpub.in
www.bookleafpub.com

Dedication

To you. Thank you.

Preface

This is a collection of life frozen in time.

Acknowledgements

Thank you to my mother, who has never given up on me.

1. Stranded

We burn brightest in the darkest of hours
and excel in the most trying of times
due to the absence of another option
or distraction that we would allow ourselves to
fall into

And in the stillness
the silent, almost peaceful, moments
I unravel
with too much space and time and things to think
Tangle myself in a web of questions
faster than I can grasp any answers

No signs are telling me which road to take
Just a fork between them and a hunger for both paths
that
leaves me stranded
here
In this place between where I've been
and where I want to be

2. Unbalanced

I've always been a bit
unbalanced
Taller and stronger than the boys my age
but not a real boy,
only those ones count
Overweight
but underfed nutrition
Under a poverty line
out of sight, out of mind
Who cares about single mothers with disabilities,
right?
Or their children
I started work at 14 to help
rather than whatever else I was meant to do

Until I slipped from the tightrope again
Fell into a pit of despair
Someone always there for me
but not always for my best interests
I always wore my seat belt

but got into the wrong cars
I didn't walk alone at night
but it was danger who held my hand
We played games of losing innocence as if
it wasn't something I could miss

I spin the wheels in my mind
over and over and over
every little thing it can conjure
Can't decide if I'm worthy
or the worst
I don't want to take this life for granted
but it seems to take so much from me

Takes so much to try and toe the lines they draw in
the sand
Be appealing, but not too revealing
Be friendly, but not a pushover
"Normal" people wouldn't do that, stop it

I hold my breath every time I leave the house
watch every step
Too easy a target if I trip
again
I try to contain myself in an orderly fashion
for your convenience
and in my weakness

Keep setting my needs down to hold yours more
easily
I wouldn't want to lose my balance

3. Sinking

My depression
turns me into an amnesiac
Every day, I forget why I'm alive
I forget who I am
I don't feel like this
is the person I am meant to be

Instead, I'm a strange awareness
a soul trapped in this body where
depression has made a home
Sinking into it without noticing it there
at first
I know it's name, at least
and try to arm myself with that
Knowledge as power
The armor piles up
My guard becomes so heavy I feel the ground beneath
give way
I sink into the fears I carry every day
too afraid to change

So strange how such solid earth can feel like quicksand
The feeling is strongest in speech with strangers
At a bar, I take a chance and go stand outside with the
"cool kids"
A particularly hot one looks at me
When he says my name it sounds foreign
When he asks me what I do, what I love
All I can manage is to point at my boyfriend and say
"That guy"

It is the sound of me choking
body being slowly swallowed by sand
I do not have time to catch my breathe and offer
a real answer
before the conversation diverts
Do not have the strength to laugh and assert myself
To tell them that I love writing and baking
That I am the caregiver of too many people
that I love too many things
And in my car days later I realize
that I am both the girl struggling to speak
and the people ignoring her
I swear to anything even resembling a god that I
know what's in here
But I'll be damned if I let her speak
At least,
that's what it seems like

I can't tell you why I am always getting in my own way
Only that I do
Or why I'm always afraid
Only that I am
But if the feeling is constant regardless
I resign myself to try regardless
of how many times I feel myself sinking

4. Unzip

Me giving you permission to grab my ass
did Not give you permission to do
the rest of what you did
Me being too shocked and uncomfortable to tell you
to stop
does Not mean I was enjoying it
Me pretending like nothing happened the next day
does Not mean I am okay with it
Truly, it means the opposite

I did not know what to do so I did nothing
I have been conditioned this way by
fear and experiences from every older man
before you
Meekness is not my soul, but my daily breakfast cereal
A habit
With a society full of examples to reinforce it

Times like this, I wish I could unzip my skin
Take off my body like a jacket to hang

forgotten in the back of a closet
Far from me
Or maybe, in a museum
So at least then when it is ogled and fantasized about
I do not need to be in the front row seat
The ghost in a one-way box
Everyone stares at all there is to see o the outside
Unable to gaze upon or acknowledge what's within
Greeted only by what they want to see against the
object's shape
The object that wanted it
Was begging for it
Deserves it
Soley for standing where it could be see

I want to disappear
So I may cease to be
an object or burden
Some prize to be won
Curse to be carried
Problem to be solved

I want to stop taking up space
around you
Because no matter how small I Feel
I know this body fills up too much room
Takes in too much air

Makes you uneasy in whatever way it can
With expression or awkward conversation
Clumsy existence

I wouldn't mind existing so much could I do so
without carrying this corpse around
Bones of rigid anxiety
Fleshy depression, deceptive in its
fair, bright beauty
Held together only because it would be
less convenient
to terminate itself
Pushed on with muscles of persistence
the good buried inside me that burns the harder I
make it work
The further I push them through this
shit-show society
That gives me the right to remain silent, in fact
it insists
Wants this body for one thing with no regards
to the host or its health

I want instead to dissolve into the moon glow that
found me beautiful in innocent, pure, timid light
To be light enough for the breeze to carry me
away from here
Far enough that nothing is familiar

and my fear may find peace in kindness unknown

5. Entomology

Every fiber of my being was screaming, “no.”
That I didn't want this, that it wasn't right
Not for me
Not now
My body was on fire
my mind trying to make it run
Make it do anything but this
I was haunted even then by the taste of regret and fear
thick on my tongue
like the blood soon spilled
But instead of resisting
instead of running or fighting or
listening to any part of myself that made sense
One word slipped from between my trembling,
chapped lips
Three little letters that changed the rest of my life
and betrayed my soul
It's what I learned to do

I'm older, not wiser

He even looks much the same as the first
As he speaks, his words strike
chord after chord
tightening in my chest
tensing in my muscles
until I feel like a coiled snake
anger, a venom in my mouth
waiting, for the right moment to strike
As he continues, I realize I am instead
tensed in place with rigor mortis
dead to the world around me
with a still tongue that will rot away in my mouth
Dull eyes seeing nothing,
that don't even tear up as he goes on
Limbs still connected
but cannot move
that will not carry me away from him

Butterfly, they've called me
and they all make sure to pin my wings in kind
Assume I am the kind of woman
they can preserve in the state of their liking
a display for their eyes, and hands, alone

No more

6. Ghost of You

Sometimes, I still feel the ghost of you
Or, feel like a ghost when I remember the part of me
that died in your presence
This haunting is my fault, I know
When I think of you though I know that I don't need to,
like-
turning out the light and saying your name
three times to a mirror
Waiting to see if the image of you will still appear
To see if it will still scare me

It's so far away now
another time and place, a different life-
like it never even happened- some days
Others, all it takes is one thing-
a song, article, face, name-
and the weight of you is crushing my ribs all over again
I stand amid the things that have come to make me feel
safe
Yet my chest is so tight I may cease breathing-

if I even am to start with-
Sometimes the thought of you makes me forget how to

After you, I relearned so many things like-
how to say "now"
How to take more responsibility and less blame
How to be okay with this person
and the shell that she lives in
How to identify with terms and labels that have nothing
to do
with you
Or what you did to me

But I wish I could learn to forget
along with this forgiveness I've found
To file you away like an old bill in the bottom drawer-
once important but no longer relevant-
nothing to think about these days

Sometimes, I wish the memory of you would vanish the
same way my self-worth did for a time
when it did when it didn't even occur to me to go
looking for it

Then again, perhaps this is better
Because my worth came back with a vengeance
with brighter colors and a stronger resolve

Whereas you remain a ghost I hope not to run into
at the grocery store
These days, I am brave enough to go inside anyway

7. Swallowed Whole

I am standing in the Wal-Mart McDonald's,
which already makes me feel dirty,
when I look over and see a man that I recognize.
That has been inside of me-
was invited but the letter was forged
by pressure of peers and conditioning under men
stronger and older and more demanding
than the body of my teenage self that feels so small now.
Felt even smaller then
beneath a question it always wanted to say
"no" to.
Funny how two tiny letters can get caught in a throat
and as my body was busy choking on my spirit
he took it
Said it was better than the last two who did the same
thing to me
"You're welcome"
As if his manliness was somehow superior
between my jail-bait thighs
"There you go girl"

As if it were any less rape-y, like...
as if
23 now, I swallow the bile and remember how many
years separate
the feeling
That I don't need to feel anything
and I'm not sure if I do
It's a strange sensation to see a man like that in the wild
Like the whale that swallowed you whole once
Left you in a dark, suffocating place you were sure you'd
never
get out of
Even if you did, how would you keep from drowning?

I feel like I have been drowning for years
Every time I think I have figured out which way is up
reach for the broken light with weak limbs
there's another wave
another whale
I watch him with the woman and child that his
proximity claims
I make sure when my order is ready
that it's me that moves beside him to take it
and not my boyfriend
I remind myself that I know how to find the shore

8. Rage

There is a quiet rage that burns deep in my core
In the face of being ignored
My center, molten and churning
My crust, so pleasing to the eye
So easy to destroy with human hands
and given the same consideration

A man once decided to hug me in line at the bank
Both arms around, crushing my side-ways body into his chest.
To soothe. Reassure.
My blood boiled for my lack of action.
For the society that made him think that was okay to do
and not okay for me to be upset about it.

Perhaps my silence has to do with this
The void my words fall into when used
Abyss threatening to swallow me whole with them
So when the next time comes
and the magma burns the back of my tongue

fighting to see the light of day
I swallow it down and live with the volcano in my belly
that every man believes to be dormant

Live with the conflicting plates of my interests and conditioning
Clashing until my internal turmoil shakes the world around it
And begins to break to the surface
The only way it knows how
And hating itself for its own nature

9. White Winter

My friends are impressed when I name White Winter
Hymnal by Fleet Foxes within only the first few seconds
of it playing
I am impressed by the way that song never fails to seize
my chest
You would think after the hundredth time or so of
listening
it would stop aching but-
That's the thing about us, isn't it?
It always hurts to think of you
It burns to turn that wheel back in time,
like the man in the music video trying to return to the
days before
Trying to melt the tension- I mean, snow
To revive memories- I mean, mushrooms
I watch them lift from the icy earth and stand on their
own again, full of life
Then, just as quickly, we are snapped back to the present
where the world is cold and it's been years since we
could

hold each others' hands
Sometimes I wonder if it's better this way
because as long as you held mine, you were never safe
Neither was I
Do you remember the time you dreamt of dying out in the snow
and the very next morning snow touched our town like it hadn't done in years?
I had never been so afraid of a white winter
I felt like that dream was my fault because the night before I placed the ring you made for me in the freezer
hoping to freeze the feelings that would not stop burning holes into my chest
I can still hear the wind blow through them
Still feel the empty space echo like winter streets
and fear that I will one day wake to the news of your death

Mykonos by the same band does it too
I don't know why his voice makes me think of you but it does
Maybe because the songs sound like longing
They make up some obscure soundtrack to the life we had together once
Taking me there every time one catches me off guard
and leaving me with whiplash

Like the hills and trees that scraped my hands and knees,
they feel like home the way that you did once
So I threw that ring into Clack Canyon when I was ready
to let go of you
And it was then that you decided to reach out to me
again
What kind of masochists are we?
I've been trying to figure out if this is a wound that
doesn't close due to its own depth
or because I keep opening it
over and over again at the sight of you
or someone that looks like you
with each song or quote about heartache as if they were
written about you and me

It's getting cold as I write this
and contemplate our life in dying light
I'm not sure what to do with it
Though our growth I do admire
soon it will be cold enough to build another fire

10. Burn Letter

I wrote you a long letter that I'll never ever send
while you were away in rehab
Seems a waste of my time, but I had to put these
thoughts
and feelings down somewhere
Shot them close range then buried them in pages and ink
I might just let a fire do away with the remains I think
Because I don't know what remains of us
what it is that we have left
or left
over the course of that month in Mesa without a letter of
goodbye
And every time I cry I find myself so frustrated at the
tears
so many have collected over the years because of you
And I feel like such a stupid little girl for everything
I've ever let you put me through

I tried asking once, why it was me you first came to love
What it was about me that made me a class above

But you just said you were a kid that didn't know any better
Like it would have been better if it were anyone else
And I realize now's the time to stop living on your back-up shelf

Stop lying awake to wait and hear you softly snoring
And take a page out of your book about forgetting and ignoring
Because this love does me no good here,
not this place time
So if it's going to stay it has to be out of sight and out of mind
Because if I lose myself again I'm afraid of what I'll find

I'm trying to figure out what the best parts of me are
Because right now it just seems like however I can be used
and how far
My love stretches,
bearing the weight and the strain
When you call me over just to help you out again
And say things that never come true
Make plans that we never go do
But still when you need me
I always come through
Sometimes I don't know what I get out of knowing you

Maybe I just needed that baseline of what not to do
What the wrong place looks like
so it's easier to tell the difference when I come to
something else

Like a man that wants to see me when he's sober
Be seen with me in daylight hours
Might even buy me flowers
just because it was me he was thinking of
I don't know
All the things people talk about in normal dating seem to
have
missed me by a mile
And now that I'm really alone I'm trying to relearn what
makes me smile
Instead of just worrying about yours
And I loved you, of course
But I think it’s time I take a turn
At loving myself first

11. 5 AM

It's 5AM and I am awoken from a dream where I had been
lying in a bed beside you
Your warmth, your scent,
enveloping me the same way they did when you were actually here
My chest aches because you're not
I message you before my brain has a chance to intercept,
heart flying from my fingertips to say...
“hey”
Seems to be the only way we can greet each other these days
Would be too out of place to say anything else
Like how I miss you in my life
or love you as deeply as I ever have
even though we can't try again
“Together” is not an option and it's not that I want to make it one
But your hands still feel like a home I cherish
Your body a safe haven-

"Sup"
- no longer
Gotta keep it casual
Like "dude"
"bro"
on the down low
Unless you ask for nudes again because you miss my
body too but
we go right back after
Where the closest I can get to telling you "I love you"
and meaning it the way I do is to tell you to be safe
"Dude" has replaced "Babe"
"Have a good day" has replaced
"Call me when you get home"
I have partners I go home to
I should not miss you like I do
But loving the sun does not change my love of the rain
I love both the same
even if I can't have both at the same time
And a tiny part of me will always be yours
even if you were never meant to be mine

12. My Heart

My heart is not unhappy where it sleeps
But still,
sometimes,
dreams of the other beds it's been in
Wishes to press against a chest from before
Feel that other heart
beat
once more
What is the word for too much love in one body?
I am a big girl
but this body is far too small for the swell of emotions
always filling it up
Afraid one day I'll just
burst from it all

My heart is always bleeding from its place on my sleeve
I'm always worried I'll out myself as the fragile
selfish thing I am
The one that cares too much about everything
Falls in loves with strangers

and remembers all those who have forgotten it
already

My heart is an adventurer
always up for a challenge
Often loving sad boys and girls miles away
Trying to give them the lighthouse kind of love
to guide them through the storms they have to
weather alone
It wishes they didn't have to be alone, but
also has trouble picturing them with anyone else
My heart often betrays me this way
Is really not the best navigator, at least
not when it comes to avoiding grief
Apparently, that's just not our thing

My heart bares the mark of every heart that has touched
it
Like a tattoo that there is just no removal for
There is no laser surgery for the soul, so
I bare the burden of the love that stays
That I cannot ask to leave because I do not know
who I am
without it
Do not have a reason to be here besides
Love
Gets me out of bed in the morning

My heart may often be heavy
Always carrying the weight of the world upon it
But baby, that is just strength training
You will not find a heart that will love yours better
That will withstand as much for simply the sake of you
What is the word for loving so deeply
despite being given every reason not to?
My heart

13. No (My Power)

There is power in the word "no"
No- a dam between the valley and the flood
between a soul and the social onslaught of
expectations, requests, and standards
A self-made source of freedom

No- a red light, stop sign, do not pass go-
to those that wish to entrap or enslave us
drain or claim us
Is the sign of most resistance
of silent no more
of reclaiming ourselves

No- both the bomb and the shelter
But my tongue has never truly crafted an explosion
Bombs are in the mind of the beholder
Someone will always regard your refusal to bend over
backwards for them
as an attack
For me, it is shelter, shield, and salve

Time to heal
A piece of myself no one can steal
after I've given too many away already
I must learn how to keep my "No" steady
Practice forming the syllable and it's sound
while I'm alone with my thoughts
Those that would drown me if I let them
slithering in my mind
"Stupid. Useless. Slut."
When I'm vulnerable
"Nothing is okay"
I say "no."
Chant it like a prayer
Like a banishing of the self that has been convinced
away from her worth
No
I will not be a victim of my disease
No
I am not an object whose purpose is to please
No
I am only responsible for me, myself, and I
No
I will unlock my power before I die

14. The Expanse

I take the weight of the world so seriously that I swear
it's what I've become
Or maybe what I've always been
A ball of passion and burning life
Covered in layers, solid and colliding
Trying to do the best I can as a hunk of stardust that has
stumbled into
sentience and is
hurling through a void that is truly endless
Without limits but living inside limits I've assigned
myself
How silly it is to simplify the magnitude of magnificence
in existence
Or dismiss the magic that is
All over an identity crisis

15. Seaside

I long for the seaside
For the feeling it stirred inside
so small beside its vastness
but so vast beside everything I was up to that day

It was there I felt God
rocking me with water
Tasting of salt
Shining like an opportunity in the ways most frightening
and telling me that it has been inside me all along

I have trouble remembering that
without sand between my toes
and its great big body, a mirror
reflecting every truth back to me
and the smell that I can only describe as freedom

I tried to bottle it
but such things cannot be contained, or shelved
We must delve into them head-first each time

But if I could have stopped time itself right then
I would have
and allowed the ocean to sing me into eternity

16. My Mother's Daughter

I feel the most like my mother's daughter while driving
especially backing out of my driveway
coffee cup in one hand
eyes all the way around and a smooth motion
Or the times that should have been an accident
but I was quick to prevent
I still remember her tea all over her lap and the dash
scared tongue lashing with anger
at the driver who can't even hear her
And must not have seen her before pushing over
Be it luck, skill, or magic
I've yet to be in a car accident while behind the wheel

I feel like my mother's daughter when that scared anger
finds me
overwhelmed and facing injustices
She has always wanted to make the world better
no matter how many times it's broken her
Has always kept her doors open to those in need
no matter how many times it's led to theft

She gives until nothing is left

I feel like my mother's daughter when I rescue
stray cats and sad humans
Feel the pain of everyone around me
When I see the wonders of nature at work
how the decay will renew
what's been lost here
We make art out of our fear
and take turns telling each other it will all be alright
It will be alright

17. Gratitude

When I think of gratitude
I picture the quiet in early morning
the calm, stillness of night
the taste of fresh air
the stars that shine bright
I think of the trees and all their strength
a cup of coffee made just right
a cozy place with a good book
and writing by candle light

I ponder the wide world's wonders
or hear the laughter of a child
Imagine a storm with crashing thunder
or magic running wild

I'm grateful for every song that has ever made me feel
to every person who has ever lent a hand
and reminded me that kindness is still real

I think of the crisis line

and my relief that they work over text
that she helped me choose to stay
despite the fear of what comes next

This life is overwhelming
can feel like only a series of hardships to survive
but it's all a the little things about it
that make me thankful I'm alive

And I know that tomorrow
the sun will rise
and we can try again

18. Beauty

When painting Beauty
include the flowers that have yet to bloom
tree branches broken in monsoon
and anything that love can be found in

When searching for Beauty
get beneath the skin
turn over rocks, go for a swim
splash around in the soul
linger by places of good deeds
sow seeds
So that more beautiful things may be found come spring
Sing to the strangers and plants and stray cats that
speckle
the streets
It might just be how you meet
Beauty
is waiting for you
but she can be shy

Sometimes catches the eye but often enjoys being more subtle
Doesn't always say hello first
She likes being recognized
Finds it
a sweet surprise

If you still aren't quite sure what you are even looking for
Beauty
is in a baby's laughter
the way it can't help but burst and bubble
is in the smile of a sweetheart
is the lullabies that can soothe both to sleep

Beauty
is the shirt off a back to a stranger
is – we'll bear this together
is no happy while you suffer
not alone
See she
is empathy
and hope
Songs above the sirens and over harsh seas
Beauty is in the resilience in spirit
is – In you

Though you may have forgotten
Though some days make it impossible to believe
Perhaps, check up your sleeve
or behind your ear
Because Beauty
has always been right here

19. Unbroken

They say to ask a potential partner questions like this one
What is your favorite animal, and three words to describe it?
Some poor girl asked and was met with "butterfly"
because, and I quote, "they are silent and pretty, easy"
A man used to call me his butterfly
And the one after, mariposa
Each one thinking I am an object to contain
That they had the right to pin my wings and mount me like a trophy
But this one,
he's a horseman
Loves them in all their challenge and personality
each quirk is something new to learn
rather than some burden to be subdued
He keeps their spirits
unbroken and true
I'm learning what it feels like to be loved
in all my flaws and spite

encouraging me to find the unbroken spirit within
me
and flourish, with all my might

20. Balanced

Life is a balancing, my love
but not an act
Keep that in the theater
in the blanket fort shows you will put on for your
future children
It will not serve you elsewhere
to act as though you are anything else but you
In all your tender, painful, vibrancy
question marked and scared,
you look like you've been places
It's okay to let others know what those places are
It's okay if you aren't ready to
but do not pretend they don't exist
because it is your foundation
your roots
reach for the sunlight exactly where you are
plants do both right?
I will photosynthesize my happiness and let myself be
nourished from the ground up
from the pain up

from the past forward
I'll be a sunflower
keeping my face to the sun as we go
round and round again

21. An Open Letter

My dear, I admit
I do not know you
but I do know that I love you
Because we bleed the same
in crimson hues, tints of hope and clumsy splotches
of insecurity
You mean the world to me
because you are a miracle that happens to breathe
the same air as I
walk along so many streets like mine
treasure, and waste, the same time
I do not know what mistakes you have made
but I know they are there
and relish in being human with you
I forgive you for each and every one
even if you struggle to forgive yourself
These days are hard for you, I know
I ache to lift the burden from you shoulders
Mend the breaks in your heart and give you something
to lean on when the very ground we tread is unstable

I wish I was able
But all we can do is grow
I will water you with my words
and hope that the light of my love helps to brighten
your days
even a little
Because I love every piece of you
Polished or jagged
Sturdy or broken
Perfectly imperfect

You are the only one like you
And I could never love anyone else the same
So I hope that you-
whoever you are
wherever you dwell
whatever you strive to be
Know that you are love in the deepest,
most encompassing way possible
Blindly, unconditionally, and without a shred of regret

Sincerely,
your friendly neighborhood humanist

www.ingramcontent.com/pod-product-compliance
Lightning Source LLC
Chambersburg PA
CBHW051737130826
49812CB00033B/900
* 9 7 8 9 3 7 0 9 2 9 7 8 4 *